REBIRTH OF FREE VERSE
SOCIETY

REBIRTH OF FREE VERSE

Society

by *j.e.Rosser*

SPRING CEDARS

Copyright © 2021 by j.e.Rosser

All rights reserved.

First edition, 2021

Cover artwork by Pamela Compton
Ironworkers, 2012, acrylic and mixed media on wood, 60 x 48 in.

Book design by Spring Cedars

ISBN 978-1-950484-12-6 (paperback)
ISBN 978-1-950484-14-0 (ebook)

Published by Spring Cedars
Denver, Colorado
info@springcedars.com

TABLE OF CONTENTS

Education	8
superhero	9
meanings	10
pimping the stature	11
made in China	12
Mortality	13
Chicago	14
sunrise in LA	16
marching	17
Holly Could if Holly Would	18
Continental Trek	20
Lost Angels	21
dominoes	22
Peachtree Perpetrator	23
New York New York	25
green scene	27
purple mountain majesty	29
talk tv	30
disclaimer	31
pills 4 U	32
Vick'me	33
break a man	35
on point	36
tour of duty	37
Spirit of Bayonet	39

Courting Calliope	41
shine	44
Decade Seasoned & Preserved With Salt	45
Vegas	51
pets	52
Case of NCAA vs. USC vs. Heisman Trophy	53
smokers	55
myPhone	56
clusters around check stand	58
Redneck	59
death of iambic pentameter	60
Waiting on Mnemosyne	61
El Cortez	62
taco	64
football father	65
kinship	68
crucified spirit	69
fate	70
ladder	71
famous	72
more	73

What do you think an artist is? An imbecile who has only eyes if he's a painter, or ears if he's a musician, or a lyre at every level of his heart if he's a poet […]? On the contrary, he's at the same time a political being, constantly alive to heartrending, fiery, or happy events, molding himself in their likeness …

—PABLO PICASSO

Education

I am the mind
of offspring born
as retribution for
carnal indulgence
delivered as bedside
burden for mother

Teach me Teacher

Reach out
with knowledge
needed on journey
to educate my mind
help me with discipline
Provide direction please

Teach me Teacher

Introduce the student
in me to person within
I cannot see but can still be
by learning to make reading
my escape from boredom
the curse of ordinary means

Teach me Teacher

superhero

movie character
hero to kids the anti
adult for adults who wait
to be rescued from boredom
of being themselves waiting
in cape & costume on other
side of adolescence held
hostage by imagination
of movie producer
who wow adults
with cartoon character
in flesh for kids created
on backlot of Hollywood
set called America where
super heroes are born for
box office to breed movies
about delayed adolescence

meanings

words can be soft as feather of dove
or callous like cracked concrete be
neath soul of inner city streets

intoxicated words flow angry from
whiskey bottle like kind words affect
sobriety untouched by drinking

words describe beauty of aurora borealis
celestial light not dimmed by darkness
while ugly words leave shade behind

words poisoned by toxic spirit destroy
with impact of nuclear bomb like words
heal wounds that otherwise last a lifetime

pimping the stature

    born in
    USA
    made
    overseas—

    satisfies
    corporate
    greed

    born in
    USA
    outsourced
    minimum pay

made in China

Corporate back door
move inflate the
dollar scheme

ship livelihoodx
of local citizen
overseas

jobs in America
exported for
foreign economy

label reads made
in China reality is
not hiring in this country

Mortality

Death
is not scared
of you dying is
what Death does

Chicago

broad
shoulders
belly of beef
Vienna smell
tempts appetite
in Chi Town
Midwest
port of call
transplanted
seed of
population
lured by
dream of
Lake Shore
Drive with
bird's eye view
from Downtown
that horizon above
concrete jungle
habitat where
huddled masses
future predicated on
zip code in metropolis
alienated by cultural
(bridges)
gather for daily passage

(bridges)
between north & south
(bridges)
border east & west
(bridges)
common to Chicago

sunrise in LA

At daybreak I confront
parasites who invade
breathing space above
Los Angeles basin to
face Tuesday marine
layer of congestion
before noon in coastal
jungle of pipe dreams
with tributaries leading
to California as last stop for
humanity before City of Angels
drowns as island on shore of America
after Big Quake is conjured by Mother
Nature as punishment for paradise West of
Eden

marching

unless life
is umbrella

death march
to grave

begins
on birthday

Holly Could if Holly Would

SUNSET BOULEVARD
Paved with shadows of fame
from journey to celebrity role
baggage at LAX left unclaimed
Lena Horne said, "It's not the load
that breaks you down—it's the
way you carry it."

Holly auditions for Tinsel Town
as tradition for talent to be found
looking for life on silver screen
face to behold—blockbuster gold
Katharine Hepburn said, "To keep
character intact you cannot stoop
to filthy acts."

Holly is in 20s world where beauty
is makeup & lights on photogenic
face—at 30 youth peels like paint
covering cracks at Chateau Alto Nido
Lucille Ball said, "Love yourself first,
and everything else falls into line."

At crossroad of ambition destiny points
East where artist grows with each audition
until in glow of Manhattan marquee fans

line up to see Holly act on BROADWAY
Grace Kelly said, "I avoid looking back,
I prefer good memories to regrets."

Continental Trek

Dressed as jock out of jersey
at Heathrow he came calling
to claim celebrity identity tarnished
by time spent on trial at Ito Court

England do not patronize California
native son the Brentwood Tabloid King
Tabloid King Brentwood Tabloid King

His need is for admiration at any cost
Behold bloody absurdity with hands not
guilty nor innocent hands forgiven by
blackface jury of peers at Ito Court

Brentwood Tabloid King Tabloid King
Brentwood Tabloid King at Heathrow
he came calling

Lost Angels

Los Angeles
famous for neon
nights on Hollywood
Boulevard—Vine Street
Queen & runaway teen

among angels
with clipped wings
no choir sings

Los Angeles
famous for Valley
porno set—cocktail
chicks with perfect
breast & kitty too pretty
to stroll turning tricks on call

among angels
with clipped wings
no choir sings on

dominoes

what are you doing
with your greatest
gift of them all

stacking
dominoes
or watching
them fall

Peachtree Perpetrator

NFL At-lanta! NFL At-lanta!
peach of Southern town At-lanta!

Millennium celebration
welcome Rams welcome Titans
Tennessee plays St Louis in
Super gridiron Sunday game

NFL At-lanta! NFL At-lanta!

football festivity
recipe for hospitality
at core of city scene
Super Bowl XXXIV

NFL At-lanta! NFL At-lanta!

night life breeds party scene
fun!—fight!—confrontation
provoke violence of Baltimore
player down Buckhead way

NFL At-lanta! NFL At-lanta!

—knife—

evidence of crime
not traceable to hand
responsible for blood from
bodies victim of weapon

NFL At-lanta! NFL At-lanta!

perpetrator escaped by
reasonable doubt—he said
she said—they said—the truth
died just another lie

NFL At-lanta! NFL At-lanta!
peach of Southern town At-lanta!

New York New York
(urban rant)

Life at core of apple pie melting pot
crust from goddamn beginning pitiful
ending home to refugee & parasite in
urban struggle to see tomorrow one day
at a time—from future fate they borrow
denied for pride is commonality

city I have to see city I have to be
city at my feet city above the street

Police here—perpetrator there—impose
will on weak one fights the other for
privilege of ruling streets of ethnic
enclaves divided by borough identity
with borders as barriers of class that
breed destiny void of upward mobility

city I have to see city I have to be
city at my feet city above the street

Thugs mock male authority
with dare fostered by indignity
even less respect validate value of
femininity forget about respect for
elderly in world that breeds crime

as birthright of family inheritance

city I have to see city I have to be
city at my feet city above the street

Are you kidding me ten cruisers
(two-deep) for resisting arrest on
code blue beat down wielding shield
to protect while in midtown walks white
collar criminal as face covered by mask
of vulture clean shaven in shirt & tie

city I have to see city I have to be
city at my feet city above the street

green scene

herbal remedy
for misery—
smoke one

crack a mickeys
drown the
sticky icky

alcohol & pill
clean scene—
smoke one

crack a mickeys
drown the
sticky icky

for holier than
thou religion—
smoke one

crack a mickeys
drown the
sticky icky

high on life
without vice—yo!

smoke one

crack a mickeys
drown the
sticky icky

antidote for mean
the green scene
icky sticky—smoke one

purple mountain majesty

got a dollar I can borrow
the uninvited asked in parking
lot of purple mountain majesty

get a job you frickin bum
people like you disgust me
you frickin stand around
walk around lay around
living off taxpayer pity
mouth open—hand out
gimme!gimme!gimme!

I frickin kiss ass eat crap
people frickin dump on me
I work for a living what
make you bottom feeders
the GODdamn chosen ones
to get something for nothing
gimme!gimme!gimme!

got a dollar I can borrow
the uninvited asked in parking
lot of purple mountain majesty

talk tv

jerry! jerry!! jerry!!!

mistress
& mayor
cincin
nati affair
social rami
fication moral
alienation

network talk
show host
prostitute
privacy
coast
to
coast

hey look at me—I'm on t v!

disclaimer

script might cause weight gain
of 100 pounds or hair could fall
out if you don't shrink 6 inches
before body turns male if female
female if male if symptoms worsen
contact physician who prescribed
medication for script to mask threat
to health of previous pills

pills 4 U
(big Pharma pushing)

script
to put you
to sleep

script
to get you
out of bed

Good Morning, Life

script
to feel good
about feeling bad

script
drug dealers
use to pacify pain

I'm here for my refill

Vick'me

I hate dogs!—loath dog lovers
now Vick'me Humane Society
make me appear to be the only
predator gone astray in culture
of animal people believe it or
not you are the same piss taking
poop dropping element as me
I hate dogs!—loath dog lovers
now Vick'me for all prosperity
you don't have to know me to
judge me just jump at the chance
to dog-me-out—you know the deal
dog-fought-dog on my watch for
dollars & hollers on my watch—dogs
died on my watch just like families
cried on my watch victim of thug
culture embodied by neighborhood
of sons & brothers as strangers who
fell dead on my watch murdered by
predators punished less than me
I hate dogs!—loath dog lovers
now Vick'me TMZ ABC NFL
scapegoat me ESPN for history of
man & dog history of dog vs dog
with money on the line never mind
it did not begin with Media coverage

as vilification validating venting of
bleeding hearts that pump opinions
like severed arteries ooze blood
I hate dogs!—loath dog lovers
now Vick'me Jane & Joe Public
with highbrow low maintenance
judgement imposed to justify my
fame—fortune—future—yeah me
assumed guilty as accused party
I hate dogs!—loath dog lovers
now Vick'me for Lassie & Rin Tin
Tin while elephants stalk donkeys
in Washington DC for head count in
political arena without scrutiny yet
you demonize an athlete as poster
boy for animal cruelty

break a man

break-a-man break-a-man break-a-man
break him!
beat-him-down beat-him-down beat-him-
down
beat him!
kick-his-ass kick-his-ass kick-his-ass
kick him!
hit him hard—hit him hard—hit him hard
hit him!
LAPD—badge LAPD—gun LAPD—club
police him!
arrest him detest him deny violence on film
defend them!
break-a-man break-a-man break-a-man
verdict!—LAPD…Not Guilty

on point

in camouflage green
me & my sweet 16

loaded—barrel—clean
came to cap the scene

me & my sweet 16
temper is unseen

'til triggered—

in camouflage green
me & my sweet 16

on point

tour of duty
(d'nam)

Dear diary

big game hunter
in eye of tiger—I hump
dressed to kill in g.i. green
with M-16—I hump

I hump I hump I hump
thru rice paddies
like river of tears—I hump
for twelve months
in terrain of fears—I hump

In-coming!!!—cover!—bunker down!!!

Dear diary

out of the mud
of monsoon months—I hump
weight of world in
rucksack on my back—I hump

I hump I hump I hump

never knowing where I'm going

hot LZ—jump!—run! VC ville
fire in the hole!—desolate hill
climb—descend—do it again

AMBUSH!!!—pray!—fire away!!!

Dear diary

to make it thru my tour of duty
I hump I hunt I bleed I kill I burn
I give I take I love I hate I'm left
blown away

my boots move on
I corp
    II corp
        III corp IV

after I die
I'm born again
an eagle's heart
with boots that grunt

Spirit of Bayonet
(Parris Island)

Go!Go!Go!—Who rule!—We rule!
4th PLATOON!—4th PLATOON!—Go!!!
circle of camouflage & green enclose
would-be Marines—Officers in waiting
occupy faceless field stripped of grass
reduced to dirt by souls of countless
boots challenged to be born again
among men on Parris Island

two girls enter—one man leaves—one man leaves
two girls enter—one man leaves—one man leaves
two girls enter—two girls enter—one man leaves
Candidates
square off
in caged helmet
pugil sticks in hand
"whistle" blows—Drill Instructor bark
commands

...square the ENEMY!—JAB!JAB!—SLASH!—
SLASH!
THRUST! JAB!!—that ain't no GODdamn Q-tip
get VERTICAL—BUTT STROKE! BUTT
STROKE!

*HEAD SHOT!—BEAT HIM DOWN—BREAK HIM!
PARRY!—SLASH!—KILL!—now!—TAKE HIM!
I said KILL! YOU SONS-OF-BITCH!...Git up!
sorry sack of shit!—git out of my GODdamn CIRcle!*

two girls enter—one man leaves—one man leaves
two girls enter—one man leaves—one man leaves
two girls enter—two girl enter—one man leaves

Courting Calliope

9th Daughter of Mnemosyne my Muse
as voice of 21st Century verse moved to
represent poetry free of esoteric rein the fall
of Bellerophon I follow to scale Mount
Olympus
between Pegasus wings destiny the realm of
poetry
to recognize journalistic hinterland on back lot
of
Hollywood set called America where
Americans
known as Californians rally around freeway
like
fashion designers on Rodeo Drive to revel in
escape of number (32) as aging celebrity jock
bolts from Brentwood hiding in back seat of
proverbial bucking bleeding Ford Bronco
driven by fellow jock out of jersey
followed
by LAPD posse with flashing emergency lights
into living rooms from Martha's Vineyard to
Lake Shore Drive providing television viewing
from Green Bay to Baton Rouge thru
lens of
camera patronizing California native son

captured for trial public affection fostered
flowers for lawyers in light
of
dark comedy
at Ito Court while commoners gathered
outside
California Criminal Court building
Downtown
to sell T-shirts with memorabilia that
advertised
The Accused on cover of magazines &
newspapers
beauty of ugliness endorsed by bookstores
banking
on related reading that glorified infamy of his
name
the trophy athlete B-grade actor in Case Of
Deadly
Vanity he became celebrity jock out of jersey
trapped
by clues visible thru lining of lies behind
curtains on
window with view to the kill at crime scene
where
evidence was collected—(hood) with hair from
head
of killer (glove)—left hand glove worn by
killer
(footprint)—size 12 Bruno Magli soles covered
with
victim's blood made roadmap in direction
taken by

killer into oblivion where Guilt was denied by Jury
blackface Jury—the conscience of Justinian at Ito Court

shine

Excuse me
this shine
is mine

Find your
own light
to shine in

Decade Seasoned & Preserved With Salt

I remember...

popular pastime inspired by vanity
known as spotting fake perfection
fake breast fake muscles fake faces
fake families *remember?* Miami Vice
influence on fashion with crumpled
wardrobe—lazy razor look with wind
blown hair *remember?* culinary void
felt deep within when realization that
sushi blackened fish & granola are for
other people's appetite—ummm! not mine
remember? home invasions by telephone
pirates ring! ring!—telemarketing scheme
from faceless voice with rainbow of gifts
for credit card digits with expiration date

I remember

crusades of redneck preachers to resurrect
Bible Belt hypocrisy with Jesus for sell
JEsus! alive in jeans moshing to lyrics of
Suicidal Tendencies—JEsus!—God said give
big live large *remember?* Media coverage
of scapegoats made celebrities of the time

like B. Goetz—Queen Leona—M. Qaddafi
Jean Harris—Bork—Zola Budd *remember?*
frequency with which Hollywood types
enhanced career longevity in twilight
years acting as pitch people 'Trust me'
honesty implied 'Would I lie to you?'
I remember
my reaction of gender alienation when
offended by shoot'um up! blow'um up!
beat'um down! exploits of bad ass white
boys inside Hollywood movie machine
created for gender superiority i.e. Tarzan
The Ape Man in '81–90 years later—why?
is all I can say—thank me later *remember?*
N.W.A. cold diss of L.A.P.D. with rap
record that rhymes with pluck the Police
remember? commercial sex on TV with
ABCs (ass boobs crotch) that sold billions
in beer—shampoo & razors along with history
for sell via big screen versions of Vietnam by
A-list directors who glorified defeat as profit

I remember

not knowing what happened to privileged
woman as wife—worker—mother who bailed
on three to be one fulltime rather than have
it all—not to be outdone by real men who
needed prenups to prevent being taken
advantage of by love *remember?* Jane
daddy's daughter need for maiden-hyphen-
married name as reminder of who wears if
not shares jockstrap in her marriage per

Daddy's approval *remember?* descent into
denial about how many of those more than
30 million idiots at large are your family
and friends—I was shocked to know

I remember

mocking those forgettable models
of femininity represented by Roseanne
Whoopie Oprah Doctor Ruth Liberace
would be remiss not to mention Vanna
Donna Fawn & Dolly *remember?* daytime
bored disease how those infected died the way
they lived vegging on the tube watching "talk"
TV *what about?* Monkey Business in Bimini
the boat—bikini—that one-piece with breast
with potential president the jackpot of tabloid
covers while Rocky ruled the big screen then
morphed into Rambo to rival Italian mark
left by Michelangelo on Western Art

I remember

foreign affairs that had America
posted on periphery of Third World
terror with Marine peacekeepers 241
memories in uniform born to families
left gripped by grief delivered in suicide
truck bomb in Lebanon *remember?* guns
for hostage scheme of renegade Colonel
wielding executive privilege at behest of
Commander In Chief asleep at the helm
when not reading cue cards for cliché in

privacy of oval office with Lady in Red
committed to Just Say No solution for
White House war on drugs

I remember

Prince William Sound 32 million gallons
of oil spilled in manmade disaster of
Exxon Valdez violation of nature along
Alaskan coast with 3rd Mate oblivious
to navigation sonar at helm while ship
Captain fell asleep in the bottle below
deck *remember?* Reagan finest hour in
'lovely little war' when freedom of press
was waived with ban on media coverage
no reporters—no cameras—no news in
clandestine operation where soldiers
armed for Nation of 300 million invaded
island of Grenada populated by 86,000
citizens of color as political coup to rescue
medical students from threat of Communist

I remember

Penthouse article about Iran Contra
that exposed players & conspiracy swept
under carpet at 1600 Pennsylvania Avenue
guarded by Republican media along with
Oliver North use of White House privilege
to finance untold kilos of Contra cocaine as
payment on guns in hands of insurgents
backed by Democracy endorsed by Teflon
Ron *remember?* lack of solidarity on behalf

of Democrats Anonymous divided by those
who could not unite The Party A(black
candidate) B(female) C(immigrant)
D(all of the above)

what about?
'Showtime' at courtside when fans came
together at The Forum inside those pillars
of Roman lore to watch basketball royalty
in purple & gold—All hail! Lakers Court!
remember? Billy Martin's Bay Area baseball
the birth of pitch'um—run'um—bash'um
style
played in Oakland by the Athletics while
across
the bay landmark magnificence of Golden
Gate
Bridge provided passage to fame for
Montana's
49ers mining gridiron glory in Candle Stick
Park

I remember

those reoccurring episodes of As The
White House Turns with televised coverage
of Republicans in revolving stained-glass
door of Reagan Cabinet members departure
'81 to '83 '84 '85–'86 '87—exodus for G.O.P.
persona non grata fate continued in '88–'89
when Ronnie & Replacements followed Lady
In Red from rose-colored glass of big white
house at 1600 Pennsylvania Avenue

I would be
remiss not to mention pride in ethnicity
inspired by bust of brother man Harold
Washington above broad shoulders of
Chicago as Mr. Mayor—cannot forget to
mention the dignity in femininity of sister
Faye Wattleton Planned Parenthood leader
same pride recognize intelligent & gorgeous
presence of Our Lady Vanessa crowned most
beautiful reincarnation of Master Jefferson's
conscience…Miss America

Vegas
(don't sleep on it)

desert valley with
mountain view
cultivated
as Las Vegas
is no mirage
time stops here
you can kiss
Lady Luck here
make love with
the moment here
Downtown—The Boulevard
escape reality for Adult Disney
leave bible at home you won't need
a watch Vegas rocks twenty-four seven

pets

with dogs & cats
I choose to not socially
interact in fact I find it
less than neighborly
when your 4-legged
family takes liberty to
dump on my property
with you in plain view

Case of NCAA vs. USC vs. Heisman Trophy
(Verdict: Give It Back)

Give it back for being California footnote to
Collegiate football history so Mr. Heisman can
Rest in peace so scrutiny can cease so USC
can
Count just 6 not 7 of his trophies that validate
Greatness equal to Southern Cal's Trojan (5)
That never happened as penalty exercised by
Powers that be to un-play 12-win Trojan
season
Payment predicated on games that were never
Played while teammates give back pain from
damage to body mind & spirit as sacrifice for
gridiron glory epitomized then despised by
NCAA for violation of rules that marginalize
personal value of number on jersey that
generate
$million$ in profit for Watch Dog—money for
everyone associated with game not in helmet
not in cleats & pads on game day like Trojan
(5)
2005 Pac 12 Champion that never was can
forget
his sacrifice of pain as pleasure rooted in
passion

for football—give it back—give back the
Trophy
so Mr. Heisman can rest in peace then
scrutiny
of Trojan football can cease

smokers

make mine marijuana

let me
catch a buzz
with my contact
cancer from your
suicidal tendency

make mine marijuana

let me trip righteous
on buzz from exhaled
trails of cancerous
pollution killing me
puff by nicotine puff

make mine marijuana

myPhone

call me if you have nothing to say
call me with minutes we'll play
call me I keep cell phone in hand
call me—or text—unlimited plan
call me before and after whatever
call me day or night I'm busy never
call me bitch to bitch dude on dude
call me in public—who said it's rude
call me—it's my right to git ignorant
call me—if you don't I git indignant
call me every minute—every 5-10
call me on landline when cell ends
call me at checkout in grocery store
call me—no!—tweet Lakers final score
call me—while on bed prepping for tan
call me—damn!—light at intersection I ran
call me when getting your nails done
call me partying at the club having fun
call me at work from 9 to 5 I'm there
call me from parking lot no matter where
call me—talk about kids—snow and mittens
call me when dog has puppies cat has kittens
call me curbside from airport as arrival dictate
call me after court date to determine your fate
call me—us talking and driving is not a crime

caller!caller!—are you there?...are you there?
caller had wreck D.O.A....nothing more to say

clusters around check stand

at closing
time Aurora Borealis
fade to black in background
of galaxy that captures celebrity
life aglow as commoners star gaze
with celestial beings consumed by
galaxy of Hollywood mania

they came—they browsed—they bought
Aurora! Aurora! Aurora Borealis!

when stars
come out to flaunt
foreplay with paparazzi
couch potatoes pine from
Manhattan to Long Island
for intimacy of Broadway
laundry on sell in Midtown

they stalk!—they trap!—they shoot!
Paparazzi makes celebrity gossip news

Redneck

Mason
Dixon line
ain't hard to
find when you
lookin away to Dixie

Till the cows come home—I'm free to roam

My America
south of Washington
D.C. a foreign place
when I look away at
peace for me in Dixie

Till the cows come home—I'm free to roam

Here is where
I stand to drive my
pick-up truck with rifle
rack—dead rabbits in back
singing sweet home Alabama

death of iambic pentameter

buried alive as print in slush pile of industry
anonymity I mingle without name recognition
on brink of suffocation pushing poems to
bottom
of the pile separating my poetry from pages
around
me without period no comma flexing verse the
anti
thesis of writing without heart & soul with
arms
connected to legs that crawl across page as
characters in black print on white space
a writer with work written in red to
bleed for the Muse the poet of
poem next in line to be read
by acquisition reader

Waiting on Mnemosyne

6 feet
4 inches
of chest
shoulders
legs & arms
pores breathing
Paco Rabanne
lying bare back
on leather couch
body in Paris briefs
waiting for date with
Mnemosyne in black
dress a dress short
tight & mini with
back out front cut to fit
curves of breast a dress
destined to rendezvous
with surrender without
conscience comfortable
in heat of passion a dress
that fills room with smell
of Aromatic Elixir the scent
Mnemosyne conjures in arrival
flaunting her little black dress

El Cortez

Mr. Porterhouse 9.99 16 oz

80's sign of the times
Downtown culture of
Fremont Street nightlife
alive along Glitter Gulch
electricity energizes escape
East of Las Vegas Boulevard
rendezvous with gambler in you
Roulette—Dice—Blackjack—Texas
Hold'em slot machines reel players
in for 777s—jackpot!—fans feast on
TV games with point spread for parlay
lounging in sportsbook you can feel
energy of live 21 single deck dealer
cocktails comped by Casino 24-7

El Cortez 6th Street & Fremont

journey to dark side
back streets begin
at Ogden lower end of
Downtown extend from Safari
Motel to Western Casino where
view is dim with fewer tourists
more local element life is cheap

down there cheap rent cheap sex
cheap drugs priced low enough
to be affordable on levels where
hourly motels & rented weeklies
do more business than souvenir
shops down on Fremont where
cars ride legs stroll past El Cortez

taco
(Arizona in me)

universal
meal in hand—

first cousin
burrito

morning
noon & night—

I grub-up
on a bite—

gimme 10
tacos

football father
(recruiting game)

position coach came calling
on mission for head coach too busy
for personal recruitment of son in
living room of home where wife and I
nurtured contempt for recruiting process
introduced with itinerary of lies (student
athlete first) (we never redshirt—except for
injury) (you get to compete
at your position) (best player plays)
(limited scholarships
prevent stockpiling)

college recruit—welcome to the game

politics of favoritism compromised
integrity of fatherly influence after
son commitment to join collection of
trophies paid promissory paper for college
education attracted by lure of college football
led me to question NCAA book of character
development for coaches if indeed there was
such a publication as guideline

rah! rah!—COL-lege FOOT-ball

I grabbed my parent play book to
research 'coach'…much to my chagrin
there was nothing on ethics for collecting
trophies of flesh not a word related to 'coach'
lying as circumstance dictates predicated on
trust to inspire commonality among boys
conditioned by men to embrace challenge
of manhood

influenced by father—chosen by coach

in parent playbook nothing
qualified 'coach' as exempt from
character development not a single
chapter in playbook for game of life
which led me to wonder what if
character to coach is spelled m-o-n-e-y
which means NCAA is just the treasury
of college football therefore eligibility has
more value than education in exploitation
of son with gift for the game

rah! rah!—COL-lege FOOT-ball

my son was not just another jock as bait
for coaching upward mobility predicated
on pecking order of players from back street
of broken homes—their blown out knees
fractured necks—the shredded muscles for
dream of life that follow college sacrifice in
NFL city—a pro player
he was not meant to be

though sacrifice was not in vain on quest for
degree from education provided with
scholarship
paid in full at graduation as student athlete

college recruit—welcome to the game

kinship

blood buys
family ties

compromise
family ties

happy disguise
family ties

hurtful lies
family ties

marital demise
family ties

jealousy realize
family ties

love despise
family ties

envious eyes
family ties

crucified spirit

scorn me
put me on
a cross
to warn me

don't claim me
crucify my soul
for death to
shame me

fate
(marbles)

into
the circle—

cat eye
spins

choosing
the hand—

it wants
to be in

ladder

ladder
to no where
twist & turn
backwards
forward
thru
darkness
it travels
nocturnally
to daylight
uphill down
stream on dry
land liquid in
solid form
destiny
intersects
with tomorrow
today parallel on
horizontal plane
leading back
to the future

famous

share your
happiness & joy
your peace of mind
the endearing times the
escape from reality to
be you—in mirror of your
life—be famous—share your
heart ache & despair the lonely
moments when drink & drug are
the light in dark corner of self
be famous—listen to praise bask in
glory of you on pedestal above reality
feed that need for attention—let fans
keep you in demand with popularity
polish your image—blow kisses to
audience—be famous

more

I had a dream
I got everything
I ever wanted in life

The nightmare was
everything I wanted
left me wanting more

VISIT
WWW.JEROSSER.COM
FOR MORE

www.ingramcontent.com/pod-product-compliance
Lightning Source LLC
Chambersburg PA
CBHW032212040426
42449CB00005B/552